EGYPTIAN TOMBS

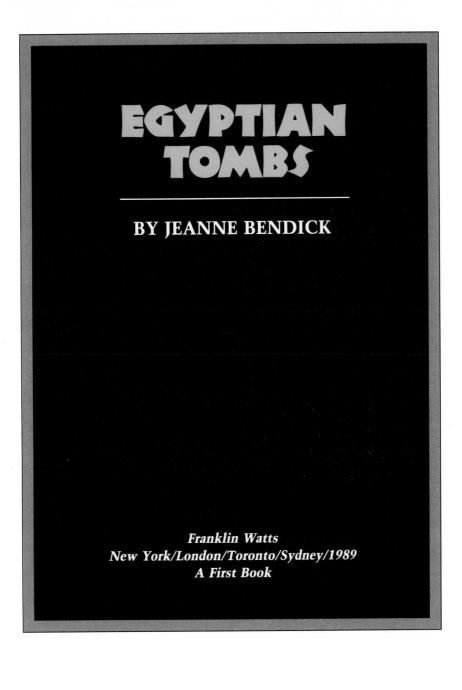

EGYPTIAN TOMBS

BY JEANNE BENDICK

Franklin Watts
New York/London/Toronto/Sydney/1989
A First Book

MANY THANKS TO
MRS. CIESIELSKI, MRS. PESCE,
AND THEIR CLASSES AT THE
HARRIS SCHOOL IN WOONSOCKET,
RHODE ISLAND, FOR THEIR HELP
WITH IDEAS FOR THIS BOOK.

Frontis: one of the golden coffins of the boy-king Tutankhamen

Cover illustration by Gary A. Lippincott

Illustrations by Jeanne Bendick
Photographs courtesy of: Art Resource: pp. 2 (Scala), 49 (Bildarchiv
Foto Marburg), 52 (left, Scala), 57 (SEF); New York Public Library
Picture Collection: p. 8; Bendick Associates: pp. 11, 18, 23 (bottom, all from "Mystery of the Pyramids"); Metropolitan Museum
of Art: pp. 14, 15, 39, 47, 48, 50, 51, 52 (right); British Museum:
p. 20; Robert Bendick: 23 (top), 28, 37 (center and bottom), 44,
59; Sheridan Photo Library: pp. 26 (B. Norman), 30; *Egypt Observed* by Henri Gougaud and Colette Gouvion, Hachette, Paris:
p. 27; Peter Clayton: p. 37 (top).

Library of Congress Cataloging-in-Publication Data

Bendick, Jeanne.
Egyptian tombs / by Jeanne Bendick.
p.   cm. — (A First book)
Includes index.
Summary: Discusses the design, purpose, and excavation of the
pyramids of ancient Egypt, the Egyptians' beliefs about death,
how mummies were made, and some legends about the pyramids.
ISBN 0-531-10462-1
1. Tombs—Egypt—Juvenile literature.   2. Pyramids—Egypt—
Juvenile literature.   3. Funeral rites and ceremonies—Egypt—
Juvenile literature.   [1. Tombs—Egypt.   2. Pyramids—Egypt.
3. Egypt—Antiquities.]   I. Title.   II. Series.
DT62.T6B46 1988
932—dc19   87-27918   CIP   AC

CONTENTS

EGYPTIAN TOMBS

*Illustration of the tale of the Great Pyramid
from the* **Arabian Nights** *collection*

AL-MAMUN AND
THE GREAT PYRAMID

More than a thousand years ago, al-Mamun (al-mah-MOON), a young **caliph** (KAY-lif) of Baghdad (BAG-dad), made up his mind to find the secret treasure that was buried in the Great Pyramid at Giza. Al-Mamun's father, Harun al-Rashid (ha-ROON al-rash-EED), was thought to be the caliph referred to in the tales of the *Arabian Nights*. One of those tales told of a wonderful treasure that had been buried in the Great Pyramid, along with Khufu (KOO-foo), the Egyptian king who had built the **pyramid** as his tomb. (Khufu was his Egyptian name. The Greeks, in their writings on the history of Egypt, called him Cheops [KEE-ops].)

PYRAMID

The story said that the treasure was much more than gold and jewels. There was also a strange metal that would never rust and a kind of glass that could bend and not break. There were charts of the stars and maps of places on earth that had not been discovered yet. There were lost secrets of science from the distant Egyptian past.

METAL

Caliph al-Mamun was a scientist himself, and he wanted those secrets more than he wanted the

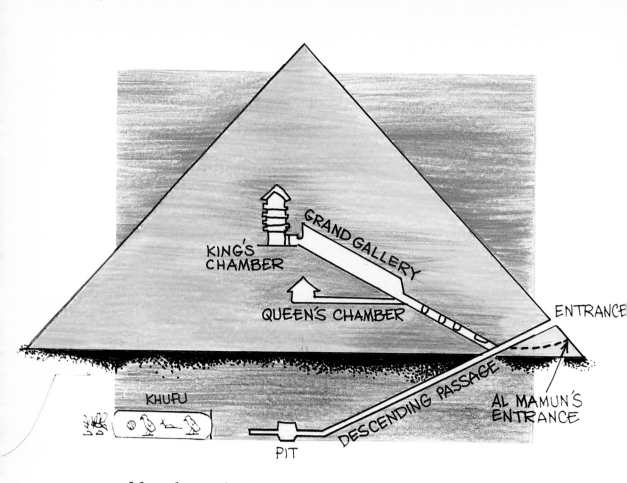

gold and jewels. So he gathered a company of engineers, builders, craftsmen, and laborers to help him find the treasure. When the expedition members arrived at the Great Pyramid they could hardly believe what they saw—a stone mountain almost 500 feet (150 m) tall and covering 13 acres. Behind this giant structure were two other pyramids almost as big and a number of smaller ones. But al-Mamun was interested only in the largest, the one that was supposed to hold the lost secrets.

Stories told of a secret door into the pyramid, leading to a secret passage, but even after weeks of searching, no door was found. Finally, the caliph decided to break his way in. The crew worked with hammers, chisels, and battering rams. They built fires to heat the stones, which cracked when they were splashed with cold vinegar. Once inside, they had to work by torchlight.

DOOR

Old engraving of Arabs coming to the Great Pyramid

For weeks they dug and hammered through the rock, trying to make a passage. They broke through into an old passage that led up to the secret outside door they had not been able to find. A low, narrow crawlway led from the door, and they followed it down and down, into the bottom of the pyramid. This passageway brought them to a small, empty room. There was another passage out of the room. It ended in a blank wall.

So they started over. And at last, after months of hacking and digging, they found a very wide passage leading up into the pyramid. Climbing up the passage on each other's shoulders they reached a big, square room built into the rock.

Khufu's burial chamber!

SARCOPHAGUS

The room was empty, except for a huge stone coffin, or **sarcophagus** (sar-COFF-ah-gus). They all rushed over and crowded around to see inside. The coffin was empty.

Where was the treasure? Where were the maps and charts, the secret writings? Where were the lost inventions? Where was Khufu's body?

RIVER NILE

No one knows. Except for the pyramid, the only things that have ever been found from Khufu's reign are two funeral boats that were buried nearby. The boats were built for Khufu to sail from his tomb, along the "other" river Nile that was said to run through the underworld.

Some people think that tomb robbers stole Khufu's body and all the treasure that was buried with him. But how did the robbers get into the pyramid and out again with all those things? Other people think that Khufu's body and the treasure are still in the Great Pyramid, buried in another place.

The three pyramids at Giza (GHEE-zah) are the most famous ones, but there are more than eighty other Egyptian pyramids. The **pharaohs** (FAIR-oh), which is what the kings of Egypt were called, built them for themselves as tombs. They started building their tombs as soon as they came to the throne, even if they were very young. They wanted to be sure everything was ready for the life they would live after they died.

LIFE

O
TO DIE

WHAT THE ANCIENT EGYPTIANS BELIEVED ABOUT DEATH

The ancient Egyptians believed that after their lives on earth were over, they lived a second, eternal life in another world underneath the Egypt above the ground. The underworld was a copy of the Egypt above. It even had its own river Nile. The Egyp-

The Egyptians believed that life in the under-world was similar to life on earth and that they would need to bring worldly objects with them.

tians believed that since life in the underworld was like life above, they ought to take with them the kinds of things they had owned and used in their first life. For important people that meant not only food and drink, clothing and ornaments, but also beds to sleep in, chairs and tables, jewelry and gold, cosmetics, and even boats to sail the underground river Nile.

Some of the things they wanted to take with them were actually stored in their tombs. Other items were carved or painted on the tomb walls. The Egyptians believed that these images would magically become real objects when they were needed, so that the dead owners could enjoy all their usual comforts. Often pictures of servants were painted on the walls of the tombs. Sometimes small servant statues called **shawabti** (shaw-AB-tee) were buried to do the work in the underworld. An ordinary person might have just a few. A king or a noble could have hundreds.

WALL

Shawabti statues, buried with the pharaohs

Life in the underworld was thought to be quite pleasant, but first you had to get there. There were many dangers along the way. There were fiends and monsters to be faced, and the Egyptians hoped they would face them bravely. Egyptian scribes wrote prayers that were often buried with the dead person. *The Book of the Dead* was a collection of magic spells, chants, and prayers that guaranteed safe passage through the underworld. It was a guidebook that described the place and gave in-

RA· THE SUN GOD

MAAT· GODDESS OF TRUTH

THOTH· GOD OF WISDOM

ANUBIS· GOD OF THE UNDERWORLD

structions about how to survive the dangers until you were safe forever.

The dangers were awful, but you didn't have to face them alone. Nobody was ever alone. The ancient Egyptians believed that everyone was born with spirit twins. One twin was called the **ba**. The ba lived in a person's body while he or she was alive and left it when the person died. But the ba didn't go far. It roamed around the tomb or the cemetery at night, lighting its way with a lantern,

NUT· SKY GODDESS

TAURT· WIFE OF SET

MUT· MOTHER OF THE WORLD

SEBEK· THE DESTROYING POWER OF THE SUN

HATHOR· GODDESS OF LOVE AND BEAUTY

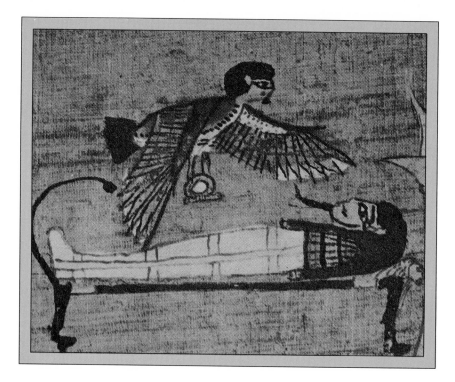

From the Book of the Dead, *an illustration of the ka coming back for its ba*

CAKE

eating the cakes that had been left for it in the tomb. Some ancient Egyptians thought that the stars were bas with their lanterns.

The other spirit twin was the **ka**. When the person was alive, the ka thought, imagined, and dreamed for its person, gave advice, and protected him or her from danger. After death, the ka stayed around inside the tomb, eating the food that had been left for it. Then it went ahead into the afterworld to prepare the way for its owner's body.

The ka came back, picked up its ba, and flew to the underworld with it. Then, for more than two months, the ba and ka roamed around, facing the dangers and looking for the god Osiris (oh-SIGH-rus), king of the dead. Osiris gave the hardest test of all, a trial in the Hall of Maat, goddess of Truth. Osiris and his forty-two assistants had the job of judging those who came before them. People had to tell their life stories before they could be admitted to the afterworld. The god Thoth (TOEth), who had the head of an ibis (EYE-bis), the sacred bird of Egypt, listened to the story and recorded it on a roll of **papyrus** (pap-EYE-rus), the paper Egyptians made from reeds.

TO FLY

TRUTH

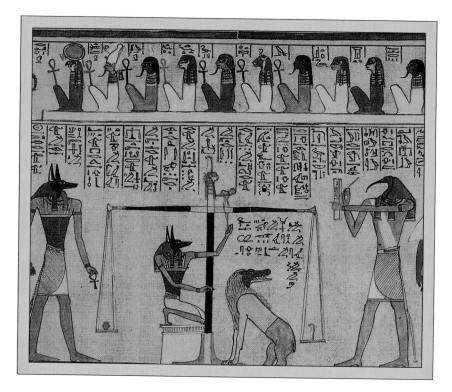

Ceremony of the heart and feather in the underworld

To test how truthful someone was, the person's heart was then weighed against a feather of Maat's. Another god, Anubis (ah-NEW-bis), who had the head of a jackal, did the weighing while a dreadful monster called the Devourer watched and waited. The Devourer had the head of a crocodile. Its front half was a lion and its rear half was a hippopotamus. People who didn't pass the test were eaten by the Devourer. But if the heart was as light as the feather, the person passed and lived happily ever after in the underworld, among friends and neighbors, pets, relatives, and ancestors.

Getting ready for death took up a lot of time during one's life on earth. But if you prepared properly, if you had lived an honest life, and if you were lucky, it was worth it.

WHAT THE ANCIENT
EGYPTIANS WERE LIKE

Six thousand years ago in Europe and in the Americas, people lived in caves or crude shelters and hunted their food with stone-tipped arrows. At the same time, however, a great civilization was growing in the valley of the river Nile.

Ancient Egypt was a fertile green strip along both sides of the river, surrounded by desert. (It is not much different today.) For thousands of years almost nobody ever crossed the desert to bother the Egyptians. They lived and prospered along

DESERT

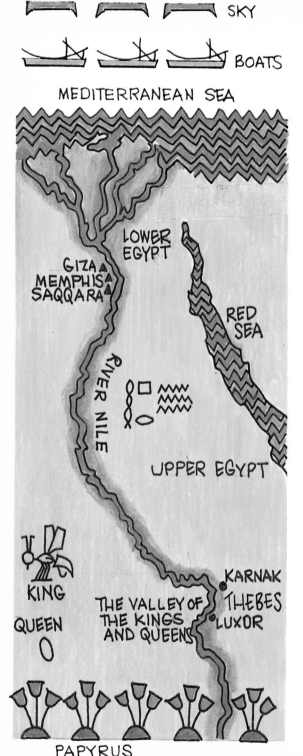

SKY

BOATS

MEDITERRANEAN SEA

LOWER EGYPT

GIZA
MEMPHIS
SAQQARA

RED SEA

RIVER NILE

UPPER EGYPT

KING

QUEEN

THE VALLEY OF THE KINGS AND QUEENS

KARNAK
THEBES
LUXOR

PAPYRUS

GROWING GRAIN

the river. They farmed and hunted and fished. They planted and harvested wheat, barley, and many kinds of fruit. They grew flax to make into linen.

Artists and craftsmen made beautiful furniture, inlaid with ivory and rare woods. They made dishes and drinking cups, pots and pans, carvings, jewelry, and ornaments. They wove linen cloth, sometimes so thin that you could see through it and sometimes so strong that it has lasted until now. They kept good records on their papyrus scrolls. They could identify and chart the important stars and foretell important events such as the yearly flooding of the Nile.

Above: *The zodiac, depicted on the ceiling of the temple of Hathor.* Below: *Farming being practiced in ancient Egypt. The scene is a detail of a wall painting in the burial chamber of Sennudem of Thebes.*

⊙
DAY

They invented a calendar of 360 days, divided into twelve months of thirty days each. The five extra days at the end of the year were feast days.

There were boat builders and sailors, artists and carpenters, weavers and astronomers. There were scientists, doctors, scribes, merchants, soldiers, masons, surveyors, undertakers, architects, and thieves. (To some Egyptians, robbing tombs was a trade.) The Egyptians built tombs, temples, and immense statues that are still there. Some Egyptian structures are among the biggest buildings on earth, even today.

Nobody is quite sure how they did some of those things. One early scientist who came to the pyramids declared that they had been built by witchcraft. And there are still people who say that the pyramids could never have been built, so long ago, without the help of intelligent beings from a faraway planet.

ℰ
ROPE

The Egyptians had no machinery. They didn't use wheels for moving loads, and they didn't have pulleys. They didn't use animals in their building work, even for hauling the tons of stone. They used wooden sledges, ropes, thousands of workers, and great skill. Because religion and death were so important in their lives, they often used these skills to build temples and tombs.

THE PYRAMIDS

The first massive stone tomb was the Step Pyramid at Sakkara (sah-KAH-rah).

KING

The Step Pyramid was the tomb of King Zoser, designed and built by his Grand Vizier (vis-YEAR) and architect, Imhotep (im-HOE-tep). The Grand Vizier was the chief officer of state. He was all the assistants that a modern head of state has rolled into one. Imhotep was so wise and talented that after he died the Egyptians declared him to be the god of mathematics, medicine, and architecture.

The Step Pyramid didn't look quite like the pyramids that came later. It looked more like a giant stone wedding cake, iced with white limestone. Imhotep built the Step Pyramid in about 2,700 B.C., and for the next five hundred years every pharaoh built himself a pyramid tomb. The pharaoh's pyramid was always the center of a group of tombs. Around it were smaller pyramids for the queens and the royal children. Other tombs in the group looked like loaf cakes. These were for the nobles. They were called **mastabas** (mas-TA-bahs), and they were like houses, some with beautifully decorated rooms inside. Below the

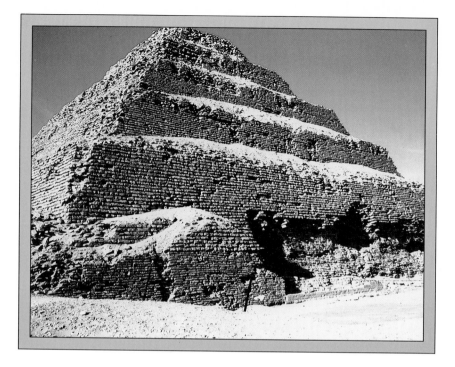

The Step Pyramid at Sakkara

rooms—sometimes far below, at the bottom of a long shaft—was the burial chamber itself. There were whole streets of mastabas around the pyramids so that the nobles could continue serving the king after they died.

A large grouping of tombs is called a **necropolis** (neh-KROP-oh-lis). The word means "city of the dead."

The interior of the mastaba
of the noble Sennufer

*The pyramids at Giza are only three of the
more than eighty built for the pharaohs of Egypt.*

The three biggest Egyptian pyramids are near
each other, at Giza. The Great Pyramid was built
for Khufu. Nearby is a slightly smaller one built
for his son, Khafre (KAH-freh). And there is a still
smaller one that was built for Khafre's son, Men-
kaure (men-CORE-reh).

The three pyramids at Giza were built near Memphis (MEM-fis), which was the royal city of Egypt for a thousand years. They are on the west bank of the Nile because west was where the sacred boat of the sun god was said to disappear every evening. (The Egyptians told of how the sun god, in his boat, simply went underground and sailed back to the east on the underworld Nile every morning.)

Building the pyramids did something more than supply the pharaohs with tombs. It gave work to hundreds of thousands of farmers who could not work their fields during the months when they were flooded by the Nile. Nile flooding was not considered a disaster. It made the Egyptian fields fertile.

Once people thought that the pyramids had been built by slaves, but many no longer believe that to be true. Some **Egyptologists** (EE-gyp-TOL-o-gists), the historians and archaeologists who study the life and customs of the ancient Egyptians, think the pyramids might have been the first great government works projects, giving employment to the farmer-citizens who were out of work.

Others think that peasants, many thousands at a time, were drafted to work on the pyramids. They probably didn't mind that much, however, because their king was thought of as a god and serving him

BUILD

The Nile, currently controlled by the Aswan Dam

was a sacred duty. On the job they had food, clothing, housing, and the pride of doing good and useful work.

HOW TO BUILD
A VERY BIG PYRAMID

You can't build a very big pyramid just anywhere. The first thing you need is a very large, flat, open space to put it on.

Second, you need a *lot* of workers. Khufu might have had about 100,000 workers at a time building the Great Pyramid. You have to build a town for your workers to live in while they are building for you and you have to supply them with food, water, and clothing. Since there are so many of them, it's helpful to have farms nearby to grow the food.

TOWN

FOOD

WATER

You need architects to design the pyramid and artists to decorate it. You need engineers to draw up the technical plans for doing the work.

You need mathematicians. Egyptians used the kind of mathematics we call **geometry**. They could not have built the pyramids without it. A Greek scientist named Thales, who lived much later, is

CLOTHING

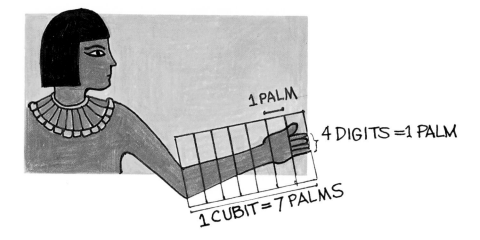

1 PALM

4 DIGITS = 1 PALM

1 CUBIT = 7 PALMS

STONE

credited with having invented geometry. Thales visited the pyramids in the fifth century, B.C. Maybe they gave him some of his ideas about geometry.

A pyramid is built of layer upon layer of huge stone blocks, laid close together. The base of the pyramid has to be exactly square, with square corners. Each layer (called a **course**) is smaller than the course below it and must be placed exactly in the middle of the course it rests on. And the upright sides of each course have to be at right angles to the ground. If any of these measurements is off, the four sides will not meet neatly at the top. So you need surveyors to lay the pyramid out and to be sure all the measurements are exact. You need overseers to see that the work is being done carefully. You need record keepers to keep track of work crews, time spent, supplies, and other expenses.

You need at least one astronomer to place the pyramid properly so that its sides face exactly north, east, south, and west. This way each face will be lit by the sun at a different season. Your astronomers will probably be priests, too.

You need a quarry where you can dig out the stone. It should be close by, because the blocks of stone are huge. Some weigh as much as 15 tons. And it has to be a big quarry. The Great Pyramid is built of 2.5 million blocks of stone.

You need a harbor for ships that bring in supplies and other building materials. Some of your supplies might be coming from other parts of Egypt, so you will have to dig canals to connect your harbor with the Nile.

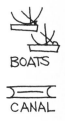

BOATS

CANAL

You need a ramp for hauling those huge stones up from the quarry to the site where you are building your pyramid. Then you will have to build another ramp on the pyramid itself, so you can drag the stones up to the level you are working on. As your workers build the pyramid higher, they have to extend the ramp. (How the ramp around the Great Pyramid looked has been a puzzle for a long

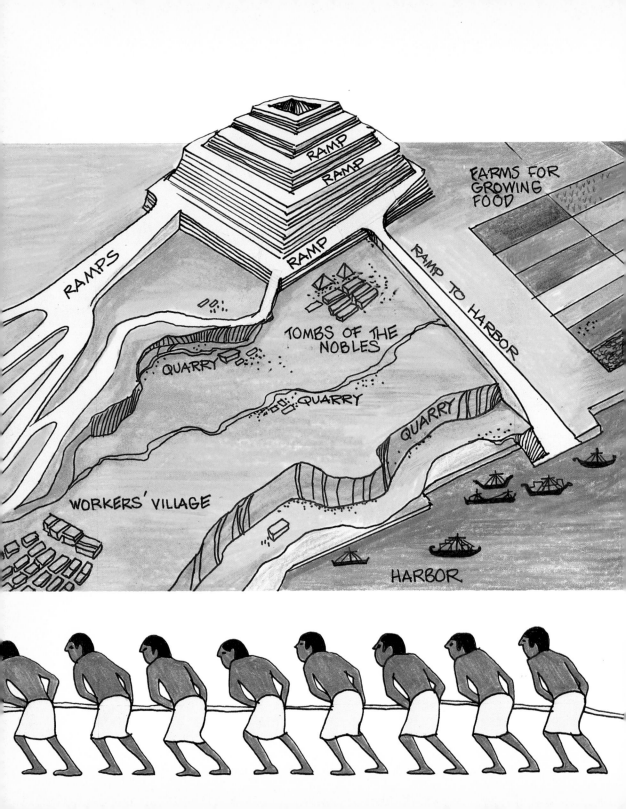

time. Now, some Egyptologists think that the ramp wrapped all the way around the Great Pyramid, up to the top. After the big, rough stones were put in place the workers covered them with thinner, smoother slabs of pale granite. These were put together so skillfully that a knife blade could not be slipped between them. The workers probably polished the outer stones on their way down and took away the ramp as they went.)

You need wooden sledges for hauling the stones and very strong ropes for pulling them up the ramps. You need many, many buckets of water for sloshing under the sledges to make them slide more easily.

You need a lot of time. Some writings say it took twenty years to build the Great Pyramid.

You need lots of resources. Some pharaohs nearly bankrupted the treasury of Egypt building their pyramid tombs.

THE SPHINX

The Sphinx (SFINX) does not seem to be a tomb. It is a statue. King Khafre had it carved out of a huge bulge of rock near the pyramids. Its body is a lion, almost as long as a football field. Its head is human—maybe a likeness of Khafre as the god Horus. (Kings supposedly became gods when they died.) Even though the Sphinx is lying down, its head is taller than a six-story building. In ancient times it was thought that the Sphinx had magic powers.

Astronomers must have chosen where to put the Sphinx because on the longest day of the year, if you stand next to the Sphinx and look toward the pyramids of Khufu and Khafre, you will see the sun setting just halfway between them. The Egyptians' writing was in the form of pictures called **hieroglyphs** (HIGH-row-glifs). One hieroglyph meant "the place where the sun sets." In this drawing, the sun seems to be halfway between two sharp mountains. Or two pyramids.

THE SPHINX
AT GIZA

Above: *the Great Sphinx of Khafre.*
Below: *for many centuries, no one
could read Egyptian hieroglyphs.
The Rosetta Stone (at left) was
the key that broke the code—
with the name Ptolemy, which
was easily recognized, being
translated into Greek letters.*

MAKING A MUMMY

MUMMY

A **mummy** is a dead body that has been preserved. The Egyptians believed that if a body was not preserved, its ka would die.

Mummification is a process of drying out. In ancient Egypt, the dead person's internal organs were removed and stored in special vases, which were then sealed. A carved scarab was put in the place of the heart. Magical writing on the scarab was supposed to keep the heart from speaking out and perhaps giving a bad impression of its owner during the heart and feather trial.

The body was dried with natron salt, then sometimes packed with spices, sawdust, or straw and a kind of glassy black stuff called bitumen, which hardened until it was almost like cement.

MUMMY
WRAPPING

Then the body was wrapped with yards and yards of linen strips that looked like bandages. The strips were wet so they could be molded to the body. Sometimes pieces of papyrus with spells written on them were slipped between the bandages. All the while, the priests chanted. There were chants for wrapping every part of the body, even for toes and fingers. Resin was sometimes poured over the whole thing. If the body had belonged to a somewhat unimportant person, the wrapping went quickly. If the mummy had been an important person, it might take months and many layers of linen to do the job properly.

Egyptians mummified the bodies of important people for more than 3,000 years. During that time, ways of making mummies varied.

The Egyptians also mummified animals. The animals might be favorite pets, whose kas would then meet the kas of their owners in the afterworld. The Egyptians liked dogs and loved cats. They also mummified sacred animals—crocodiles, ibises, rams, hawks, baboons, jackals, cows—those animals associated with Egyptian gods and goddesses.

After the body was wrapped and properly chanted over, the priests put it into a wooden mummy case shaped to fit it. A likeness of the

A mummy from 1025 B.C.

OSIRIS

ISIS AND HORUS

THE STORY OF
THE FIRST MUMMY

Osiris and his sister-wife, Isis, were king and queen of the gods. But Osiris' wicked brother Set was jealous of their happiness. He cut Osiris into fourteen pieces and hid the pieces all over Egypt. Isis searched everywhere and with the help of Thoth, the god of magic and wisdom, collected the pieces. Then Anubis, the jackal god, put the pieces together, wrapping them in place with strips of linen. Only Osiris' hands stuck out of the mummy wrappings, and in these he held the royal scepters of Egypt.

Thoth brought Osiris back to life, but Osiris the mummy could not go back to the real world. So he stayed in the underworld, where he became the god of eternal life and the judge of all those who died.

person inside was carved or painted at the top end of the mummy case. Sometimes the rest of the case was beautifully decorated with bas, kas, flowers, animals, and written prayers. Finally, the mummy case was put into a stone sarcophagus in its tomb. The stone cover was sealed, and the mummy was supposedly protected forever after.

FLOWER

But that's not what happened.

THE TOMB ROBBERS

No treasure has ever been found in any of the pyramids, even though everyone was sure that it was buried with the pharaohs. That was the trouble to begin with. Everyone knew that those tombs were full of treasure. They were a challenge and an invitation to thieves.

The kings wanted to protect the treasures they were taking with them to the afterworld. They were also concerned with protecting their mummies. After all, the mummies had to be safe if their bas and kas were to live in comfort forever. So the pyramids were designed to hide both the treasures and the mummies.

The tombs were made like giant puzzles. The

entrances were hidden. Passages were blocked with huge stones that filled them completely. Other stones were balanced so that they would crash down onto anyone who passed once the tomb was sealed. Some passages ended in blank walls or empty rooms.

PRIEST

SOLDIER

Each necropolis had a settlement of guards and priests whose only job was to take care of the tombs. Still, when archaeologists have dug and even blasted their way into those tombs, they have been found empty. They were all robbed, maybe thousands of years ago. Some tombs were robbed many times.

How could that have happened? It took al-Mamun months to get into the Great Pyramid, and he made a lot of noise while he was breaking in. He came thousands of years after the tomb was built, but the tomb had been guarded for many years. Wouldn't those guards have heard tomb robbers at work? Wouldn't they have seen them coming out with the loot?

The answer seems to be that the priests and guards, and probably the workers who built the tombs, plotted with the tomb robbers. They knew where the secret doors were, where the real passages were, and where the mummies and the treasures were hidden. This knowledge was probably passed down from generation to generation. A few of the pharaohs tried to put a stop to that by killing the people who designed the tombs. But there were always others who knew the secrets.

For many centuries the kings were buried in pyramids and the pyramids were always robbed. Finally, it became clear that a pyramid, right out in the open, was like a showcase for treasure. Robbers knew that if they were clever enough, or if they had the plans of the pyramid, all they had to do was help themselves.

THE VALLEY OF THE KINGS

About 1,500 B.C. a pharaoh named Tuthmose (TOTH-mose) decided that he would do things differently. He would put his tomb in a secret place, hidden away where the robbers couldn't find it. By this time the capital city had been moved from Memphis to Thebes, farther up the Nile. Across the river from Thebes, on the western side of the Nile, there is a rocky desert full of cliffs, stone hills, and caves. Why not cut rooms and corridors into the cliffs, big enough to hold the treasures and the mummies, and then hide the entrances so that nobody could find them?

THEBES

*View of the Valley of the Kings,
near the entrance to King Tut's tomb*

QUEEN

So many pharaohs were buried in that rocky area that today it is called the Valley of the Kings. There are hundreds of other rock-tombs where the nobles were buried. At the southern end, there are more tombs for the royal wives and mothers. That area is called the Valley of the Queens. Other tombs hold thousands of mummified ibises and baboons, animals sacred to the god Thoth.

At first, the tombs in the Valley of the Kings were simple. Then they became more complex. Flights of steps led down from the entrances; the stair walls were carved or painted with figures in a grand parade. The pictures show many different things about life in ancient Egypt.

STEPS

Stairs and ramps led down into bigger and bigger rooms until they ended up in a hall deep under the ground where the king's sarcophagus rested. The tombs of some of the nobles were just as grand as those of some of the kings.

ROOM

The first pharaohs who built their tombs in the Valley of the Kings capped them with little pyramids of brick. But even those little pyramids acted as markers, pointing to the burial places. Later cave entrances were hidden in the barren piles of rock around them. There were secret passages and even fake coffin rooms.

Between the Valley of the Kings and the Valley of the Queens there was a workers' village, where the overseers, stonecutters, masons, carvers, artists, and their families lived. The village was completely cut off from the outside world, so that the people who worked on the tombs couldn't give the tomb locations away. Everything they needed, even food, water, and firewood, was brought in to them. They were not allowed out of the valley. But none of this did any good at all. The robbers were just as successful as they had ever been. All the tombs were robbed and emptied. All but one.

THE TOMB OF KING TUT

About 1,350 B.C. a boy about nine years old, named Tutankhamen (toot-an-KAH-mon) (Tut, for short) came to the throne. He died when he was eighteen. Tut wasn't an important king, so his tomb wasn't very grand, and the things he would take with him to the afterworld were jammed and piled into four smallish rooms.

TOMB

Thousands of years went by. Other tombs were stripped bare, but nobody found Tut's tomb. At some time, many years ago, thieves did get into the first two rooms, but for some reason they didn't break into the others. Probably, they were interrupted. Most people forgot the boy king had ever existed.

THE NAME OF TUTANKHAMEN

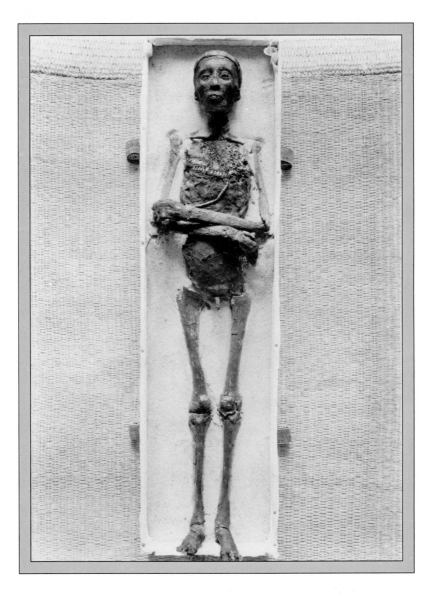

The skeleton of King Tut

In 1922 Howard Carter, a British Egyptologist, found the tomb. His heart sank when he went through the first two doors and found that the long passage had been entered. There were broken objects scattered everywhere. But the entrance to the next room was still sealed! Carter made an opening in the plaster wall, put his eye to the hole, and gasped. When he and his helpers got into that room, they found four chariots, some gilded couches, a golden throne, piles of chairs, a chest of royal robes, musical instruments, jewelry, ornaments, bows and arrows, dried foods, and many boxes full of the things that a king would need in his afterlife.

CHARIOT

THRONE

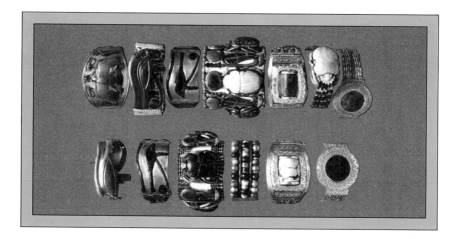

*Many exquisitely crafted bracelets
were found in the tomb.*

*A golden throne found in the tomb,
showing King Tut and his young bride*

It took four months of careful work to clear and sort all the things in that one room. At last, Carter felt free to explore the burial chamber itself. Its door was in the far wall, guarded by two life-size statues of the young king. Carter made another hole to look through, and at first he saw what he thought was a wall of gold. The treasures inside were dazzling.

The far wall of the antechamber, with two guards in the likeness of King Tut, contained the door leading to the burial chamber.

*Howard Carter brushes some dust off
the nose of the magnificent sarcophagus
found in Tut's burial chamber.*

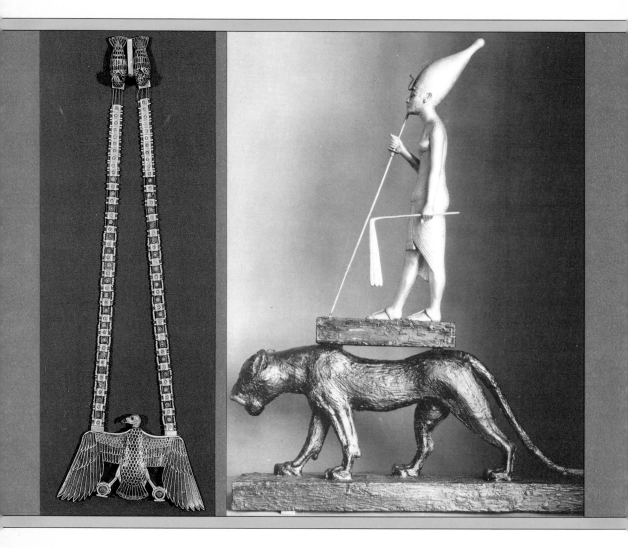

*A necklace with vulture pendant and a statuette
of the boy-king on a black leopard were among the
many treasures found in the tomb.*

Tut's sarcophagus was inside a nest of four gold boxes—real gold. On Tut's face was a solid gold mask, inlaid with semiprecious stones. There were gold and ebony shrines in the room, gold beds and chairs, alabaster boxes, sun boats, statues, jewelry, and boxes and baskets of food, all piled on top of each other, crammed into the small room.

More than three thousand objects were found in King Tut's tomb. It took more than ten years for Carter and his helpers to catalog and preserve the king's belongings so they would survive away from that sealed tomb, out in the world. Today, the treasures fill several long galleries in the world-famous Cairo Museum.

But Tutankhamen was an unimportant pharaoh. What treasures do you think might have been in the tombs of the famous pharaohs?

SPOOKY STORIES AND CURSES

Over the years, many spooky stories have been told about the pyramids and the other Egyptian tombs. Some stories said that the tombs were full of poisonous serpents, or that anyone entering would

SERPENT

have to fight bats as big as people. Other stories told of ghosts that appeared at sunrise and sunset.

There have always been stories warning of curses upon anyone who disturbed the mummies in their tombs. Those stories started again after Howard Carter entered King Tut's tomb, because some of the people in the group who worked with him died suddenly, soon after the tomb was opened. However, Howard Carter lived to be an old man.

Tomb robbers didn't worry about ghosts or curses. They didn't care a fig about the mummies being sacred, either. Sometimes they even broke up the mummies for firewood—after they had taken their jewelry, of course.

Not all the priests were in cahoots with the grave robbers. Many were loyal to their god-kings and worried about what would happen to the mummies if the grave robbers found them. So these priests secretly moved the mummies far from the treasure that the thieves were looking for. Some of the mummies were moved several times. One cave that was opened in the Valley of the Kings had no treasure but had been used to store forty royal mummies. Another cave had a dozen mummies, crammed in with some of the things that the loyal priests thought their rulers were going to need in the afterworld.

THE TOMBS
ARE STILL THERE

After the pyramids had been around for a while, they became just part of the scenery, like mountains or rivers. Wealthy Greeks and Romans visited them when their countries conquered Egypt, but the Egyptians didn't think of them as anything special. If they needed stones to build new buildings, they often took the stones from the pyramids.

NOSE, BREATH

Many statues, now, have no noses. Once in a while a pharaoh would chip the noses off all of the statues of the pharaoh who had ruled before him, so that pharaoh's ka couldn't interfere in matters of state. People believed that if a statue's nose was gone, the ka of that person would die because it couldn't breathe. But most statues have no noses because they simply broke off.

Sands drifted over the Sphinx many times, and parts have crumbled away. But there were always people to rescue it. Tuthmose IV may have been the first to restore it, about 3,500 years ago. He dreamed he had promised the Sphinx he would do that if he became pharaoh. Over the years restorers dug the sand away from the Sphinx's body and

These giant stone statues at Karnak in Egypt all show their faces crumbling or with noses broken off.

paws. They filled in cracks and rebuilt, with stone, the parts that were crumbling. When the Turks and then Napoleon conquered Egypt, their soldiers used the Sphinx and the grand statues in the temples for target practice.

With the passing years, sand drifted up over the temples. Roofs fell in; people built their houses against the walls and used the great halls for marketplaces.

Starting in the nineteenth century, almost four thousand years after the tombs were built, archaeologists began digging them out and partly restoring them, so people today can begin to see what ancient Egypt was like.

TO SEE

CLIMBING UP

Now, travelers from all over the world come to visit the tombs and temples. You can climb up the inside of the Great Pyramid. The passages are so narrow that you can touch the walls on either side. If you are tall, you have to bend over to keep from bumping your head on the rocky ceiling. On your way up to Khufu's burial chamber, you can almost feel the weight of those millions of tons of rock over your head. You can look at Khufu's empty sarcophagus and imagine how al-Mamun felt when he finally reached that room.

You can climb down steep flights of stairs, down into the tombs in the Valleys of the Kings and

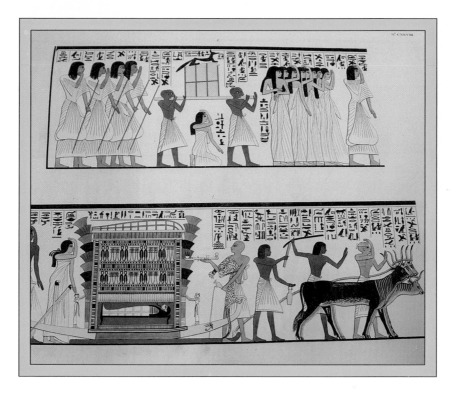

On your way down into the tombs, you are greeted by a parade of ancient Egyptians on the walls.

Queens, down to where the noble Egyptians were buried. On the way down you are part of the parade of ancient Egyptians on the walls.

There are probably more tombs still to be found. Archaeologists now have new ways to look for hidden tombs. They use a technology called **remote**

sensing. Radar and sonar are both remote-sensing technologies. So is an instrument called a **magnetometer** (mag-net-AH-mit-er), which is a little like the metal detectors people use to look for lost coins or other metal objects.

Remote sensors work by sending out signals that go underground—through sand, rocks, and soil, or even the stones inside a pyramid. Wherever there is a cave or a tomb in the rock, or a room in a pyramid, the signal will be reflected back to the searcher to show where it is.

HIDDEN

Using remote-sensing instruments, French and Japanese search teams have found hollow places in the Great Pyramid at Giza and underneath the Sphinx. Maybe the treasure of Khufu is still in one of these hidden places.

Using a magnetometer, scientists have located a lost tomb in the Valley of the Kings, near the tomb of Ramses II (RAM-seez). Archaeologists believe that it may be the tomb of some of Ramses' sons. Ramses II was one of Egypt's greatest kings, and since the tomb itself is buried behind a huge pile of rock and rubble, archaeologists hope that even the tomb robbers could not get to it. If Tut's tomb was rich, imagine the treasure that could be in the family tomb of a pharaoh as grand as Ramses II! It might even satisfy al-Mamun.

GLOSSARY

Ba. One of the spirit twins that everyone was said to be born with. The ba lived in a person's body while he or she was alive and left it at death.

Caliph. A ruler in the ancient Middle East.

Course. A single layer of stone in a pyramid.

Egyptologist. An historian who studies the life and customs of the ancient Egyptians.

Geometry. A branch of mathematics. The ancient Egyptians must have used it to design the pyramids. Thales, a Greek scientist, is credited with having invented geometry much later.

Hieroglyphs. Picture drawings that were the writing of the ancient Egyptians.

Ka. One of the spirit twins a person was born with. When the person was alive, the ka thought, dreamed, gave advice, and protected its person. After the person's death, the ka went into the underworld to prepare the way.

Magnetometer. An instrument for remote sensing (see entry) of metal objects.

Mastabas. Small, houselike tombs built for the nobles.

Mummy. A dead body that has been preserved by natural or artificial means.

Necropolis. A large grouping of tombs. The word means "city of the dead."

Papyrus. The paper Egyptians made from reeds. After it was written on, papyrus was usually rolled into a scroll.

Pharaoh. What a king of Egypt was called.

Pyramids. Steeply sloping four-sided stone buildings built as tombs for the pharaohs and their families.

Remote sensing. A way of locating something that is out of sight or hearing. Radar and sonar are examples of remote sensing.

Sarcophagus. A big stone coffin that held another coffin that held a mummy.

Shawabti. Small statues of servants often buried with the pharaohs and the nobles. The word means "answerers."

INDEX